Analogies
Quick Starts

Author: Linda Armstrong
Editor: Mary Dieterich
Proofreaders: Alexis Fey and Margaret Brown

COPYRIGHT © 2020 Mark Twain Media, Inc.

ISBN 978-1-62223-822-4

Printing No. CD-405054

Mark Twain Media, Inc., Publishers
Distributed by Carson-Dellosa Publishing LLC

Visit www.carsondellosa.com

Table of Contents

Introduction to the Teacher

To succeed in today's competitive environment, students must improve their thinking skills. Quality classroom instruction remains the cornerstone of any instructional program, but experienced teachers know all learning requires reinforcement.

This book offers teachers and parents short quick start activities to help young thinkers practice their craft. Used at the beginning of a language arts, science, spelling, geography, math, or health time slot, these mini-tasks help students focus on thinking and problem-solving skills.

The units covered include topics such as vocabulary, phonics, literature, science, geography, health, art, music, and math. Each page features two to four quick starts.

Several types of analogies commonly appear on tests, and they are used here within the subject contexts. These include the following: part to whole (*finger to hand*), object to class (*apple to fruit*), object to action (*dog to bark*), synonym (*little to small*), antonym (*little to big*), sequence (*first to second*), and object to description (*banana to yellow*). These types are introduced in the first set of exercises.

> Before distributing the exercises, explain to students that colons (:) are used in a special way in analogies. For example, "big is to large as little is to small" is written
> big : large :: little : small.

There are many ways to use this book:

- Reproduce the pages, cut along the lines, and use each section as a ten-minute warm-up or part of a homework assignment.

- Distribute copies of uncut pages so students can keep their completed exercises in a three-ring binder for reference.

- For use at a learning center, reproduce each page, cut the exercises apart, and mount each on a card with the corresponding answer key on the back. Laminate for durability.

- Make transparencies or Powerpoint™ slides for group lessons.

Note: Share the exercises in any order that fits your ongoing program.

Solving Analogies

Solving Analogies: Related Pairs 1

How is each pair of words related? Circle the best description.

1.	big : little	synonyms	antonyms
2.	finger : hand	part/whole	object/description
3.	morning : noon	object/use	sequence (order)
4.	fall : break	cause/effect	object/place
5.	scissors : cut	person/action	object/action
6.	boxer : punch	whole/part	person/action
7.	herd : cow	member/group	group/member
8.	cold : freezing	synonyms	antonyms
9.	shovel : dig	object/use	person/action
10.	racecar : fast	object/action	object/description

Solving Analogies: Related Pairs 2

Match each word pair to the correct relationship.

_____ 1. tall : short
_____ 2. apple : fruit
_____ 3. small : little
_____ 4. banana : yellow
_____ 5. brush : paint

a. object/class
b. object/action
c. antonyms
d. synonyms
e. object/description

Solving Analogies: Related Pairs 3

Use the clue to unscramble the second word in each pair.

synonyms   1. slender : htni
_____

antonyms   2. tiny : gheu
_____

sequence   3. one : wot
_____

whole/part   4. house : lwal
_____

object/class 5. snake : peerlit
_____

Solving Analogies

Solving Analogies: Related Pairs 4

Use the clue to fill in the missing letters in the second word in each pair.

person/action   1. teacher : t _ _ _ hi _ g

person/object   2. teacher : m _ _ ke _

object/action   3. marker : ma _ _

degree   4. small : t _ _ y

member/group   5. fish : sc _ _ _ l

Solving Analogies: Related Pairs 5

Use the clue to fill in the correct word.

acting	sentence	fry	sixth	laugh

cause/effect   1. joke : _____

part/whole   2. word : _____

person/action   3. actor : _____

sequence   4. fifth : _____

object/use   5. pan : _____

Solving Analogies: Related Pairs 6

Use the clue to come up with your own word to correctly complete the word pair.

synonyms   1. happy : _____

member/group   2. quarterback : _____

object/description 3. tree : _____

place/object   4. castle : _____

whole/part   5. piano : _____

Vocabulary Analogies

Vocabulary: Object/ Characteristic 1

Circle the best choice to complete the analogy.

1. banana : yellow :: plum :
   white   purple   pink
2. apple : red :: lemon :
   yellow   purple   blue
3. grapes : purple :: cantelope :
   blue   red   orange
4. lime : green :: cherry :
   green   red   blue
5. peach : orange :: strawberry :
   red   black   yellow

Vocabulary: Object/ Characteristic 2

Fill in the missing letters.

1. cactus : spiny ::
   rose : _ _ _ _ n _
2. glass : clear ::
   wood : o _ _ q _ e
3. velvet : soft ::
   steel : h _ _ _
4. sandpaper : rough ::
   foil : sm _ _ _ _
5. feather : light ::
   lead : h _ _ _ y

Vocabulary: Object/ Characteristic 3

Using the first part of the analogy as a clue, unscramble the last word in each analogy.

1. beach : warm :: mountains :
   _____ ocol
2. poles : icy :: equator :
   _____ tho
3. cottonball : fluffy :: marble :
   _____ nysih
4. cream : smooth :: apple :
   _____ rcpsi
5. night : dark :: day :
   _____ glhit

Vocabulary: Object/ Characteristic 4

Fill in the missing word.

strong	hot	cold	cool	liquid

1. ice : solid :: water : _____
2. fire : hot :: ice : _____
3. breeze : gentle :: wind : _____
4. blanket : warm :: fan : _____
5. arctic : cold :: tropics : _____

Vocabulary Analogies

Vocabulary: Object/ Characteristic 5

Match each word to the correct analogy.

a. sour   b. spicy   c. fruity
d. salty   e. sweet

1. lemon : sour :: candy : _____

2. sugar : sweet :: fries : _____

3. chips : salty :: chili : _____

4. juice : fruity :: lime : _____

5. salsa : spicy :: plum : _____

Vocabulary: Member/Group 1

Circle the best choice to complete the analogy.

1. student : class :: teacher :
   pride   herd   faculty

2. fish : school :: person :
   crowd   pride   pack

3. card : deck :: star :
   school   galaxy   corps

4. mountain : range :: wolf :
   pack   troop   swarm

5. lion : pride :: sailor :
   herd   den   crew

Vocabulary: Member/Group 2

Fill in the correct word.

senate   team   audience colony   collection

1. cookie : batch ::
   coin : _____

2. member : club ::
   senator : _____

3. grape : bunch ::
   ant : _____

4. bee : swarm ::
   listener : _____

5. employee : staff ::
   player : _____

Vocabulary: Member/Group 3

Match each word to the correct analogy.

1. dish : set :: whale : _____

2. stamp : collection :: kangaroo : _____

3. ship : fleet :: bird : _____

4. sheep : flock :: cow : _____

5. horse : herd :: rabbit : _____

a. mob   b. warren
c. pod   d. herd
e. flock

Vocabulary Analogies

Vocabulary: Member/Group 4

On your own paper, write each analogy in words. (Example: sheep : flock :: horse : herd is written as "sheep is to flock as horse is to herd".)

1. tree : grove :: flower : bed
2. actor : cast :: singer : chorus
3. chapter : book :: room : building
4. block : neighborhood :: neighborhood : city

Vocabulary: Member/Group 5

Fill in the blanks to complete the analogy.

1. cheerleader : squad ::
   musician : b _ _ d
2. firefighter : company ::
   athlete : t _ _ _
3. computer : network ::
   book : l _ _ r _ ry
4. kitten : litter :: buffalo : h _ _ d
5. tree : orchard ::
   vine : v _ _ _ y _ _ d

Vocabulary: Object/Action 1

Use the clue to unscramble the last word in each analogy.

1. glass : shatter :: rubber :
   _____ cebonu
2. top : spin :: skate :
   _____ olrl
3. snake : slither :: toad :
   _____ hpo
4. cat : pounce :: dog :
   _____ ubnod
5. wind : blow :: rain :
   _____ alfl

Vocabulary: Object/Action 2

Circle the best choice to complete the analogy.

1. finger : touch :: eye :
   hear   feel   watch
2. bell : toll :: horn :
   toot   ring   scream
3. lightning : flash :: thunder :
   ring   sing   rumble
4. scissors : cut :: spoon :
   cut   stir   paste
5. leaves : shake :: waves :
   ocean   water   break

Vocabulary Analogies

Vocabulary: Object/Action 3

Fill in the correct word from the choices in the box.

1. teeth : chew :: nose : _____
2. smoke : billow :: water : _____
3. grasshopper : hop :: mosquito : _____
4. clock : tick :: door : _____
5. snow : drift :: hail : _____

creak
flow
pelt
sniff
fly

Vocabulary: Object/Action 4

Draw a line to match each word to the correct analogy.

1. bubble : drift :: ball :   **swim**
2. balloon : rise :: anchor :   **honk**
3. bee : sting :: skunk :   **sink**
4. frog : hop :: fish :   **spray**
5. duck : quack :: goose :   **bounce**

Vocabulary: Object/Action 5

Fill in the missing letters to complete each analogy.

1. bird : sing :: frog : cr __ __ k
2. donkey : bray :: horse : __ e __ __ h
3. horse : trot :: duck : w __ __ __ l __
4. phone : ring :: horn : __ o __ __
5. knife : slice :: fork : pi __ __ __ e

Vocabulary Analogies

Vocabulary: Part/Whole 1

Circle the best choice.

1. tine : fork :: blade :

       spoon   knife

2. bristle : brush :: tread :

       tire   car

3. sleeve : shirt :: buckle :

       hat   belt

4. sole : shoe :: crystal :

       watch   table

5. key : piano :: string :

       guitar   flute

Vocabulary: Part/Whole 2

Match each word to the correct analogy.

  a. leg   b. shoe   c. head
  d. foot   e. highway

1. sidewalk : street :: shoulder : ___
2. fingers : hand :: toes : ___
3. brim : cap :: heel : ___
4. nose : face :: hair : ___
5. elbow : arm :: knee : ___

Vocabulary: Part/Whole 3

Fill in the missing letters.

1. page : book :: shelf : li _ _ a _ y
2. nostril : nose :: lip : m _ _ t _
3. floor : room :: field : s _ _ d _ _ m
4. toe : sock :: finger : g _ _ v _
5. cover : book :: lid : b _ _

Vocabulary: Part/Whole 4

On your own paper, write each analogy in words. (Example: drawer : dresser :: shelf : bookcase is written as "drawer is to dresser as shelf is to bookcase".)

1. frame : picture :: fence : yard
2. knob : drawer :: handle : door
3. piece : puzzle :: letter : word
4. mattress : bed :: burner : stove
5. inch : foot :: foot : mile

Vocabulary Analogies

Vocabulary: Part/Whole 5

roof	music	cabinet	branch	compass

Fill in the best word.

1. hand : clock :: needle : _____
2. pixel : image :: note : _____
3. needle : bough :: leaf : _____
4. glass : window :: shingle : _____
5. drawer : dresser :: door : _____

Vocabulary: Object/Purpose 1

Circle *T* for true or *F* for false about each analogy.

1. pen : write :: envelope : enclose   T   F
2. pan : cook :: soap : slice   T   F
3. towel : dry :: television : write   T   F
4. water : drink :: flashlight : light   T   F
5. food : eat :: marker : mark   T   F

Vocabulary: Object/Purpose 2

Use the clue to unscramble the last word in each analogy.

1. pool : swim :: bed : _____   lsepe
2. brush : paint :: mop : _____   elnac
3. crayon : color :: cup : _____   rdkni
4. glasses : see :: headphones : _____   lstnie
5. camera : photograph :: dryer : _____   yrd

Vocabulary Analogies

Vocabulary: Object/Purpose 3

Circle the best choice to complete the analogy.

1. shovel : dig :: box :

    write   eat   contain

2. pail : fill :: shirt :

    run   wear   sing

3. broom : sweep :: tack :

    drink   believe   hold

4. chair : sit :: nose :

    hear   smell   see

5. lamp : illuminate :: ear :

    see   hear   taste

Vocabulary: Object/Purpose 4

Fill in the missing word from the choices in the box.

clean   smooth   add   print   sew

1. scissors : cut :: needle :

    _____

2. ruler : measure :: file :

    _____

3. fork : eat :: printer :

    _____

4. staple : fasten :: toothbrush :

    _____

5. glue : stick :: calculator :

    _____

Vocabulary: Object/Purpose 5

Fill in the missing letters.

1. eraser : erase :: detergent :

    _ _ s _

2. marker : mark :: car : d _ i _ _

3. pencil : write :: food : _ _ t

4. book : read :: platter : s _ _ v _

5. money : pay :: fan : c _ _ _

Vocabulary: Synonyms & Antonyms 1

Circle the synonym that best completes the analogy.

1. total : sum :: flat :

    hilly   level

2. purpose : goal :: great :

    ordinary   grand

3. fury : rage :: happy :

    glad   miserable

4. answer : reply :: exclaim :

    declare   ask

5. begin : start :: halt :

    stop   run

Vocabulary Analogies

Vocabulary: Synonyms & Antonyms 2

Circle the missing antonym that completes the analogy.

1. love : hate :: like :

    erlmdislikekjwer

2. entertain : bore :: play :

    qazxworkatwb

3. boy : girl :: man :

    fdeascwomanmoutr

4. husband : wife :: father :

    opeymothercixzon

5. open : close :: give :

    kuewnvtakewetupm

Vocabulary: Synonyms & Antonyms 3

Fill in the missing synonym to complete the analogy.

| loyal country winner |
| site restore |

1. change : alter :: renew :

    _____

2. village : town :: place :

    _____

3. city : metropolis :: nation :

    _____

4. careful : cautious :: faithful :

    _____

5. answer : solution :: victor :

    _____

Vocabulary: Synonyms & Antonyms 4

Fill in the missing letters in the antonyms that complete each analogy.

1. happy : sad :: joyful :

    d _ _ r _ ss _ d

2. tragic : comic :: cry : l _ _ _ h

3. enemy : friend :: dislike : l _ k _

4. lose : gain :: give : t _ _ e

5. white : black :: colorful :

    color _ _ _ _

Vocabulary: Synonyms & Antonyms 5

Use the clue to unscramble the last synonym in each analogy.

1. distant : far :: close :

    _____ earn

2. revise : correct :: mature :

    _____ rogw

3. right : correct :: error :

    _____ estamik

4. story : tale :: poem :

    _____ eersv

5. large : big :: small :

    _____ tillet

Vocabulary Analogies

Vocabulary: Homophones 1

Circle the missing word.

1. ate : eight :: won :

   zero one single

2. dear : deer :: bare :

   reveal show bear

3. blew : blue :: read :

   orange red yellow

4. meet : meat :: bred :

   slice bread from

5. hole : whole :: peace :

   piece slice dove

Vocabulary: Homophones 2

Draw a line to match the word to the analogy.

1. mist : missed :: past :   **site**

2. made : maid :: hare :   **nose**

3. pause : paws : clause :   **passed**

4. cent : sent :: cite :   **claws**

5. clothes : close :: knows :   **hair**

Vocabulary: Homophones 3

On your own paper, write each analogy in words. (Example: mail : male :: sail : sale is written as "mail is to male as sail is to sale".)

1. oar : ore :: soar : sore

2. here : hear :: herd : heard

3. heal : heel :: real : reel

4. lead : led :: read : red

5. peek : peak :: week : weak

Vocabulary: Homophones 4

Use the clue to unscramble the last word in each analogy.

1. pain : pane :: main :

   _____ amne

2. tail : tale :: sail :

   _____ laes

3. toad : towed :: road :

   _____ rwedo

4. who's : whose :: you'll :

   _____ luey

5. right : write :: read :

   _____ rdee

Vocabulary Analogies

Vocabulary: Homophones 5

Use the choices to fill in the correct word.

1. be : bee :: aunt : _____   sister   relative   ant

2. beat : beet :: carat : _____   carrot   jewel   weight

3. two : to :: four : _____   eight   for   quarter

4. knew : new :: knot : _____   tie   know   not

5. pole : poll :: role : _____   roll   actor   part

Vocabulary: Suffixes 1

Circle the word with the suffix that best completes the analogy.

1. comfort : comfortable :: perish :   perished   find   perishable

2. teach : teacher :: work :   worker   play   worked

3. write : writer :: read :   reading   red   reader

4. act : actor :: edit :   editor   acting   editing

5. sell : seller :: buy :   purchase   buyer   buying

Vocabulary: Suffixes 2

Write the missing word to complete the analogy.

1. create : creative :: act : _____

2. enjoy : enjoyment :: excite : _____

3. hope : hopeless :: life : _____

4. truth : truthful :: fear : _____

5. slave : slavery :: brave : _____

Vocabulary Analogies

Vocabulary: Suffixes 3

On your own paper, write each analogy in words. (Example: slow : slower :: quick : quicker is written as "slow is to slower as quick is to quicker".)

1. strength : strengthen ::

   length : lengthen

2. light : lighter :: dark : darker

3. lucky : luckier :: happy : happier

4. soft : softest :: hard : hardest

5. boy : boyish :: girl : girlish

Vocabulary: Suffixes 4

Match each word to the correct analogy.

1. use : useless :: age : _____

2. brother : brotherly :: sister : _____

3. weary : weariness :: happy : _____

4. fearless : fearlessness :: artless :

   _____

5. kind : kindness :: dark : _____

   a. darkness   b. artlessness
   c. sisterly   d. ageless
   e. happiness

Vocabulary: Suffixes 5

Fill in the missing letters.

1. friend : friendship :: citizen:

   _ _ _ _ _ _ _ ship

2. good : goodness :: sad :

   sad _ _ _ _

3. friend : friendly :: sad : _ _ _ ly

4. laugh : laughing :: cry : cry _ _ _

5. add : addition :: divide :

   divis _ _ _

Vocabulary: Prefixes 1

Underline the word with a prefix that completes the analogy.

1. invent : reinvent :: write :

   reportnlkrewrite

2. active : inactive :: complete :

   termincompletereact

3. believe : disbelieve :: appear :

   resdisappeardislike

4. fiction : nonfiction :: profit :

   plortbsnonprofitonfelk

5. pay : repay :: fund :

   funnyfindrelayrefundpay

Vocabulary Analogies

Vocabulary: Prefixes 2

Draw a line to match each word with the correct analogy.

1. view : preview :: heat :   **misunderstand**

2. national : international :: state :   **preheat**

3. done : overdone :: spend :   **recopy**

4. read : misread :: understand :   **interstate**

5. appear : reappear :: copy :   **overspend**

Vocabulary: Prefixes 3

Write the missing word with a prefix that completes each analogy.

1. way : subway :: marine : _____

2. circle : semicircle :: finals : _____

3. healthy : unhealthy :: true : _____

4. cover : undercover :: ground : _____

5. heat : overheat :: price : _____

Vocabulary: Prefixes 4

Unscramble the last word in each analogy.

1. polite : impolite :: patient : pimnatiet _____

2. sensitive : insensitive :: perfect : ipecmerft _____

3. responsible : irresponsible :: regular : ulrraiegr _____

4. mature : immature :: possible : isiblsmpoe _____

5. visible : invisible :: attention : iionnatentt _____

Vocabulary Analogies

Vocabulary: Prefixes 5

Fill in the missing letters.

1. select : preselect :: cut :

    pre _ _ _

2. arrange : rearrange :: pay :

    _ _ pay

3. lock : unlock :: solved :

    _ _ solved

4. last : outlast :: perform :

    _ _ _ perform

5. weekly : biweekly :: annually :

    _ _ annually

Vocabulary: Greek & Latin Roots 1

Circle the best choice.

1. photograph : light :: phonograph :

    camera   film   sound

2. bicycle : two :: tricycle :

    five   three   wheel

3. telephone : hearing :: television :

    sight   distant   monitor

4. telescope : far :: microscope :

    large   vision   small

5. hemisphere : half :: biosphere :

    life   study   two

Vocabulary: Greek & Latin Roots 2

Fill in the blank to complete the analogy.

1. pedestrian : walker :: equestrian : _____

2. telegraph : write :: telephone : _____

3. quadruped : feet :: quadrangle : _____

4. friction : rubbed :: fraction : _____

5. dentist : tooth :: podiatrist : _____

6. milliliter : liquid :: milligram : _____

7. postpone : time :: postscript : _____

8. psychology : mind :: anatomy : _____

solid
foot
body
corners
speak
broken
rider
writing

Vocabulary Analogies

Vocabulary: Greek & Latin Roots 3

Match each word to the correct analogy.

1. tripod : foot :: triangle : ___

2. unicycle : wheel :: uniform : ___

3. manicure : hand :: pedicure : ___

4. insecticide : kill :: insectivore : ___

5. construct : build :: conscript : ___

   a. eat b. shape c. write
   d. foot e. corner

Vocabulary: Greek & Latin Roots 4

Fill in the missing letters.

1. nativity : birth ::

   mortality : de _ _ _

2. solar : sun :: lunar : m _ _ n

3. eject : out :: inject : _ _

4. maternal : mother :: paternal :

   fa _ _ _ r

5. import : in :: export : _ _ _

Vocabulary: Greek & Latin Roots 5

Unscramble the last word in each analogy.

1. export : carry :: extend :

   trchest _____

2. junction : join :: donation :

   geiv _____

3. altimeter : height :: barometer :

   rresepsu _____

4. minimum : less :: maximum :

   meor _____

5. oratory : speek :: auditory :

   rahe _____

Vocabulary: Clipped Words 1

Circle the best full word that completes the analogy featuring clipped words.

1. ad : advertisement :: memo :

   mention motion memorandum

2. gas : gasoline :: flu :

   influenza fluent virus

3. tux : tuxedo :: vet :

   vegetable veterinarian doctor

4. burger : hamburger :: lab :

   place laboratory scientist

5. Web : World Wide Web :: Net :

   hairnet intelligence Internet

Vocabulary Analogies

Vocabulary: Clipped Words 2

Fill in the missing letters.

1. phone : telephone :: copter :

   _ _ li _ _ p _ _ r

2. photo : photograph :: teen :

   t _ _ n _ g _ r

3. gym : gymnasium :: fan :

   fa _ _ t _ _

4. cab : taxicab :: van :

   ca _ _ v _ _

5. exam : examination :: dorm :

   do _ _ it _ _ _ .

Vocabulary: Clipped Words 3

Match each word to the correct analogy.

1. auto : automobile :: math : _____

2. auto : automobile :: bike : _____

3. lunch : luncheon :: fridge : _____

4. fax : facsimile :: lube : _____

5. asst. : assistant :: ft. : _____

   a. lubricate
   b. foot
   c. bicycle
   d. mathematics
   e. refrigerator

Vocabulary: Clipped Words 4

Write the correct word on the line.

1. copter : helicopter :: auto :

   _____

2. limo : limousine :: stereo :

   _____

3. pants : pantaloons :: tie :

   _____

4. champ : champion :: doc :

   _____

5. plane : airplane :: bus :

   _____

| necktie doctor omnibus automobile stereophonic |

Vocabulary: Clipped Words 5

Unscramble the word that completes the analogy. Write it on the line.

1. ref : referee :: grad :

   _____ agrteadu

2. rhino : rhinoceros :: hippo :

   _____ipothusopapm

3. deli : delicatessen :: sub :

   _____ bsunemari

4. quake : earthquake :: prof :

   _____ roprsofes

5. piano : pianoforte :: cell :

   _____ lulacelr

Vocabulary Analogies

Vocabulary: Acronyms 1

Circle the best choice to complete the analogy.

1. ATM : machine :: ASAP :

   after   never   possible

2. ESL : language :: EU :

   union   ever   usual

3. CD : disc :: DJ :

   juice   Denver   jockey

4. SUV : vehicle :: SOS :

   sunny   ship   over

5. TLC : care :: DVR :

   recorder   cover   very

Vocabulary: Acronyms 2

Match to complete the anaolgy.

a. view   b. computer
c. operandi   d. war
e. vehicle

1. VIP : person :: POW : _____

2. PTA : association :: POV : _____

3. PS : script :: RV : _____

4. PR : relations :: PC : _____

5. RSVP : plait :: MO : _____

Vocabulary: Acronyms 3

Fill in the missing letters.

1. NASA : administration :: PIN :

   n _ m _ _ r

2. LOL : loud :: MRI :

   i _ _ g _ _ g

3. HQ : quarters :: IQ :

   q _ _ t _ _ _ t

4. FBI : investigation :: IRS :

   s _ _ v _ c _

5. HIV : virus :: FYI :

   i _ _ o _ _ a _ _ _ n

Vocabulary: Acronyms 4

Unscramble. The word may be any word in the acronym.

1. BLT : tomato :: CEO :

   _____ oerffic

2. ERA : rights :: CIA :

   _____ ielnenctlige

3. PA : public :: HQ :

   _____ adhe

4. CEO : executive :: DVD :

   _____ idvoe

5. COD : cash :: GPA :

   _____ readg

Vocabulary Analogies

Vocabulary: Acronyms 5

Underline the missing word that completes each analogy.
The word will be the word represented by the last letter in each acronym.

1. ZIP : plan :: RAM : rowpkmomemorystem

2. RIP : peace :: TBA : beginameannouncedstand

3. UFO : object :: UPS : puposservicereceiver

4. RADAR : range :: SCUBA : belowunderapparatustable

5. SASE : envelope :: SWAT : winterseasonteamlaterafter

6. NBA : association :: NFL : longleaguelaterloseflower

7. RN : nurse :: CNA : associationnursingassistantassortment

8. DOD : defense :: HUD : developmentdepartmentunderneath

Vocabulary: Portmanteau Words 1

Portmanteau words are new words made up of a combination of two or more other words. In each analogy, you will either be looking for one of the original words, or you will be given a word and asked to find the portmanteau word.

Circle the best choice to complete each analogy.

1. glamping : camping :: infomercial :   commercial   artificial   special

2. cosplay : costume :: frenemy :   French   friend   find

3. cinema : cinemaplex :: emotion :   Internet   message   emoticon

4. liger : tiger :: brunch :   lunch   crunch   dinner

5. Frankenfood : Frankenstein :: docudrama :   film   book   documentary

Vocabulary Analogies

Vocabulary: Portmanteau Words 2

a. software	b. spatter
c. communication	d. stumble
e. rash	

Match to complete the analogy.

1. blog : log :: brash : _____
2. beefalo : buffalo :: bumble : _____
3. camcorder : recorder :: freeware : _____
4. glitz : ritz :: splatter : _____
5. hazmat : materials :: intercom : _____

Vocabulary: Portmanteau Words 3

a. snort	b. short
c. complex	d. element
e. care	

Match to complete the analogy.

1. Internet : network :: Medicare : _____
2. motel : hotel :: multiplex : _____
3. pang : sting :: pixel : _____
4. scrunch : crunch :: skort : _____
5. smog : fog :: chortle : _____

Vocabulary: Portmanteau Words 4

Fill in the missing letters.

1. guesstimate : estimate :: infomercial : c _ _ m _ r _ _ _ _
2. telethon : marathon :: sitcom : _ o _ _ _ y
3. Skylab : laboratory :: slang : l _ _ gu _ _e
4. slosh : slush :: smash : m _ _ _
5. grumble : rumble :: glop : s _ _ p

Vocabulary: Portmanteau Words 5

On your own paper, write each analogy in words. (Example: blog : log :: Internet : network is written as "blog is to log as Internet is to network")

1. squiggle : wiggle :: telethon : marathon
2. pulsar : star :: bionic : electronic
3. stagflation : inflation :: netiquette : ettiquette
4. swipe : sweep :: splatter : splash
5. carjack : hijack :: chillax : relax

Grammar Analogies

Grammar: Irregular Verb Forms 1

Circle the best choice to complete each analogy.

1. am : are :: was :   have   is   were
2. build : built :: catch :   release   caught   trap
3. feed : fed :: freeze :   froze   thaw   cold
4. fight : fought :: bring :   brought   brang   bringed
5. do : did :: get :   gave   obtain   got

Grammar: Irregular Verb Forms 2

Fill in the missing letters to complete the anaolgy.

1. eat : ate :: has : h _ _
2. draw : drew :: fly : _ _ _ w
3. forgive : forgave :: drink : dr _ _ _
4. hit : hit :: cut : _ _ t
5. light : lit :: bite : _ _ _

Grammar: Irregular Verb Forms 3

Draw lines to match the words to the correct analogy.

1. do : did :: eat :   **felt**
2. bend : bent :: bleed :   **bled**
3. choose : chose :: drink :   **broke**
4. dig : dug :: feel :   **drank**
5. forget : forgot :: break :   **ate**

Grammar Analogies

Grammar: Irregular Verb Forms 4

Unscramble the word to complete each analogy.

1. lay : laid :: lie : _____ yal

2. run : ran :: say : _____ isda

3. see : saw :: sell : _____ dlso

4. shoot : shot :: shake : _____ osokh

5. swim : swum :: spin : _____ upsn

Grammar: Irregular Verb Forms 5

Circle the missing word to complete each analogy.

1. know : knew :: grow :   groweddgrewgrowt

2. hear : heard :: make :   makedmademaidmaker

3. ride : rode :: rise :   risedrosereddrice

4. shake : shook :: take :   takedtooktakerteektike

5. has : had :: mean :   meantmeanedmeand

Grammar: Parts of Speech 1

Unscramble the word to complete each analogy with the adverb form of the word.

1. noisy : noisily :: lazy : _____ zilayl

2. rare : rarely :: nice : _____ nelyic

3. jealous : jealously :: needless : _____ ednelelyss

4. legal : legally :: internal : _____ lntinaerly

5. bashful : bashfully :: delightful : _____ dehltfulligy

Grammar Analogies

Grammar: Parts of Speech 2

Circle the missing word to indicate the part of speech.

1. table : noun :: go :

    adjectiveverbnoun

2. yellow : adjective :: slowly :

    pronounverbadverb

3. walk : verb :: path :

    nounadjectiveverb

4. loudly : adverb :: loud :

    adverbadjectivenoun

5. good : adjective :: well :

    verbadjectiveadverb

Grammar: Parts of Speech 3

Fill in the word that completes each analogy.

1. loud : loudly :: good : _____

2. quick : quickly :: slow : _____

3. happy : happily :: merry :

    _____

4. hungrily : hungry :: greedily :

    _____

5. sloppily : sloppy :: crazily :

    _____

greedy	well	crazy
slowly	merrily	

Grammar: Parts of Speech 4

Match to complete the analogy.

1. careful : carefully :: hopeful :

    ____

2. easily : easy :: wearily : ____

3. bright : brightly :: bad : ____

4. usually : usual :: helpfully : ____

5. deeply : deep :: kindly : ____

    a. kind
    b. helpful
    c. weary
    d. hopefully
    e. badly

Grammar: Parts of Speech 5

Fill in the missing letters to indicate the part of speech.

1. gentle : adjective :: gently :

    a _ _ _ _ b

2. love : noun :: lovable :

    _ d _ _ c _ i _ _

3. peacefully : adverb :: peace :

    n _ _ _

4. rider : noun :: riding : _ _ r _

5. tight : adjective :: tighter :

    a _ _ e _ _ _ v _

Phonics Analogies

Phonics: Long & Short Vowels 1

Fill in the word to complete each analogy.

1. man : mane :: pan : _____

2. van : vane :: plan : _____

3. mate : mat :: rate : _____

4. past : paste :: star : _____

5. kite : kit :: bite : _____

6. cope : cop :: hope : _____

7. trip : tripe :: snip : _____

8. sine : sin :: wine : _____

Phonics: Long & Short Vowels 2

Draw a line to match the word with the correct analogy.

1. hid : hide :: rid :   **spine**

2. grim : grime :: slim :   **slime**

3. dim : dime :: prim :   **pine**

4. fin : fine :: spin :   **prime**

5. shin : shine :: pin :   **ride**

Phonics: Long & Short Vowels 3

Unscramble the missing word in the analogy.

1. twin : twine :: grip :

    _____ ipgre

2. quit : quite :: sit :

    _____ itse

3. rob : robe :: glob :

    _____ gelob

4. hop : hope :: slop :

    _____ peslo

5. not : note :: tot ::

    _____ teot

Phonics: Long & Short Vowels 4

On your own paper, write the following analogies in words. (Example: bit : bite :: kit : kite is written as "bit is to bite as kit is to kite".)

1. hug : huge :: cut : cute

2. slat : slate :: scrap : scrape

3. gap : gape :: tap : tape

4. ton : tone :: mop : mope

5. spit : spite :: fir : fire

Phonics Analogies

Phonics: Long & Short Vowels 5

Circle the best choice to complete each analogy demonstrating the correct vowel sounds.

1. hate : hat :: cane :   candy   can   walking

2. car : care :: far :   fare   near   distant

3. cap : cape :: tap :   hit   touch   tape

4. glad : glade :: mad :   made   angry   maddening

5. grad : grade :: fad :   dance   fade   fashion

Phonics: Blends & Digraphs 1

Circle the missing word to complete the analogy.

1. blue : true :: blend :   black   mix   trend

2. cheat : treat :: chip :   piece   trip   chocolate

3. tree : flee :: try :   fly   succeed   true

4. snow : glow :: snob :   snow   glob   superior

5. stop : shop :: store :   shore   shop   stop

Phonics: Blends & Digraphs 2

Fill in the missing word to complete the analogy.

1. now : snow :: nap : _____

2. his : this :: hen : _____

3. rim : trim :: rail : _____

4. hip : ship :: hop : _____

5. car : scar :: core : _____

Phonics Analogies

Phonics: Blends & Digraphs 3

Draw a line to match the word to the correct analogy.

1. low : slow :: lid :   **gray**

2. mall : small :: mash :   **plot**

3. lace : place :: lot :   **knob**

4. new : knew :: nob :   **smash**

5. rain : grain :: ray :   **slid**

Phonics: Blends & Digraphs 4

Fill in the missing letters.

1. grad : grand :: lad : l __ __ d

2. cat : cast :: mat : m __ __ t

3. wit : with :: bat : b __ __ __

4. rig : ring :: wig : w __ __ __

5. pat : past :: wet : w __ __ __

6. ben : bench :: hen : h __ __ __ __

7. too : tooth :: boo : b __ __ __ __

8. kin : king :: tin : t __ __ __

9. we : welt :: be : b __ __ __

10. win : wing :: thin : t __ i __ __

Phonics: Blends & Digraphs 5

Circle the missing letters. The letters will be the blend or digraph found in the second word in the analogy.

1. telescope : sc :: asleep :   trsxbbsletyoon

2. muskrat : sk :: sunshine :   istyryattresshoe

3. April : pr :: respect :   ispoltruckngshmr

4. destroy : st :: patrol :   ngrtesplntrenmon

5. father : th :: singer :   pltrockngldltrd

Literature Analogies

Literature: Poetic Devices 1

On your own paper, write the following analogies in words. (Example: cricket : chirp :: chick : cheep is written as "cricket is to chirp as chick is to cheep".)

1. horse : neigh :: dog : bow-wow
2. pig : oink :: duck : quack
3. frog : ribbit :: cat : meow
4. cow : moo :: sheep : baa
5. donkey : heehaw :: chicken : cluck

Literature: Poetic Devices 2

Match the word to the correct analogy.

1. snore : zzzzzzzz :: sneeze : ____
2. clock : tick :: door : ____
3. bored : ho-hum :: laugh : ____
4. water : gurgle :: fire : ____
5. explode : boom :: guitar : ____

a. knock   b. crackle
c. twang   d. haha
e. achoo

Literature: Poetic Devices 3

Fill in the missing letters in these rhyming words.

1. late : rate :: low : r _ _
2. fought : bought :: fudge :
   b _ d _ e
3. mush : rush :: mow : r _ _
4. house : mouse :: hound :
   m _ _ _ d
5. dust : trust :: duck : tr _ _ _

Literature: Poetic Devices 4

Use the clue to unscramble the second word in each pair.

1. dear : hear :: net:
   _____ tpe
2. funny : money :: had :
   _____ dda
3. clean : mean :: bag :
   _____ arg
4. alliteration : beginning :: rhyme :
   _____ den
5. paragraph : prose :: stanza :
   _____ moep

Literature Analogies

Literature: Poetic Devices 5

Circle the best choice to complete each analogy. The words are associated with sounds.

1. disappointed : boo :: cold :   hot   chilly   brrrrh

2. doorbell : buzz :: handbell :   bronze   ding   tower

3. scared : eek :: train :   chug   railroad   plane

4. cheer : hurrah :: quiet :   song   shhh   sound

5. tasty : yum :: distasteful :   tasty   unpleasant   yuck

Literature: Narrative Elements 1

Circle the best choice to complete each analogy. The words are associated with telling a story.

1. Charlotte : character :: farm :   plot   setting   climax

2. desert : setting :: argument :   conflict   character   protagonist

3. school : setting :: Harry :   setting   time   character

4. loneliness : problem :: friendship :   resolution character   setting

5. found : resolution :: lost :   character   plot   problem

Literature: Narrative Elements 2

Fill in the word to complete each analogy. The words are associated with telling a story.

1. Charlotte : farm :: character : _____

2. poverty : wealth :: problem : _____

3. setting : store :: problem : _____

4. Harry : character :: unappreciated : _____

5. future : setting :: Merlin : _____

| poverty |
| character |
| problem |
| setting |
| resolution |

Literature Analogies

Literature: Narrative Elements 3

Match the word to the correct analogy.

1. school : setting :: Ramona : _____

2. humor : genre :: gratitude : _____

3. mystery : genre :: London : _____

4. fantasy : genre :: battle : _____

5. Huck : character :: rescue : _____

    a. setting   b. resolution
    c. conflict   d. character
    e. theme

Literature: Narrative Elements 4

Fill in the missing letters.

1. separated : problem :: reunited :

    r _ s _ l _ tion

2. Dorothy : character :: fantasy :

    g _ _ re

3. love : theme :: fight :

    c _ _ _ li _ t

4. separation : problem ::

    Land of Oz : se _ _ i _ g

5. country : setting :: Scarecrow :

    c _ _ r _ _ t _ r

Literature: Narrative Elements 5

Unscramble the letters to complete the analogy.

1. Alice : character :: Wonderland :

    _____ tinsetg

2. loss : problem :: recovery :

    _____ etiorsolun

3. midnight : setting :: greed :

    _____ tehem

4. survival : problem :: historical :

    _____ enrge

5. love : theme :: breakup :

    _____ ficctonl

Literature: Parts of a Book 1

Circle the best choice to complete each analogy.

1. name : person :: title :

    number   book

2. chapter : book :: sentence :

    paragraph   letter

3. definition : glossary ::

    page number :

    index   place

4. alphabetical : index :: sequence :

    order   contents

5. index : end :: introduction :

    conclusion   beginning

Literature Analogies

Literature: Parts of a Book 2

Fill in with the best choice to complete each analogy.

1. preface : before :: appendix :

    _____

2. book : chapter :: heading :

    _____

3. clothes : person :: cover :

    _____

4. information : chapter :: definition :

    _____

book	**glossary**
after	**subheading**

Literature: Parts of a Book 3

Match the word with the correct analogy.

1. word : dictionary :: map : _____
2. sentence : paragraph :: chapter :

    _____
3. film : narration :: picture : _____
4. town : overlook :: subject : _____
5. map : atlas :: statistics : _____

a. almanac
b. caption
c. book
d. encyclopedia
e. atlas

Literature: Parts of a Book 4

Fill in the missing letters to complete the analogy.

1. poetry : prose :: fiction :

    _ _ _ fict _ _ n

2. anthology : collection :: novel :

    f _ c _ _ _ n

3. sign : street :: guideword :

    d _ _ t _ _ n _ _ y

4. biography : nonfiction :: map :

    di _ _ r _ m

5. drawing : model :: map :

    gl _ _ e

Literature: Parts of a Book 5

Unscramble the word to complete the analogy.

1. book : catalog :: topic :

    _____ iexnd

2. encyclopedia : guide word :: Internet :

    _____ rkodeyw

3. history : nonfiction :: fantasy :

    _____ ctifino

4. glossary : vocabulary :: bibliography :

    _____ esursoc

Science Analogies

Science: Sequence 1

Circle the best choice.

1. clay : shale :: sand :

   particle   beach   sandstone

2. limestone : marble :: shale :

   slate   hard   sedimentary

3. magma : basalt :: ash :

   volcanic   porous   tuff

4. sand : sandstone :: shell :

   organic   marine   fossil

Science: Sequence 2

On your own paper, write the following analogies in words. (Example: fruit : seed :: seed : sprout is written as "fruit is to seed as seed is to sprout".)

1. seed : sprout :: sprout : stem

2. pollen : seed :: seed : sprout

3. leaf : bud :: bud : flower

4. light : photosynthesis ::

   photosynthesis : food

5. bud : flower :: flower : fruit

Science: Sequence 3

Complete each analogy with the best word.

1. rain : puddle :: wind : _____

2. rising : vapor :: cooling : _____

3. warm : rises :: cool : _____

4. cloud : charge :: lightning : _____

5. precipitation : evaporation ::

   evaporation : _____

   a. condensation
   b. replaces
   c. thunder
   d. dry
   e. cloud

Science: Sequence 4

Fill in the missing letters to complete the analogy.

1. sunrise : noon :: noon :

   s _ _ _ _ t

2. full: quarter :: crescent :

   n _ _

3. new : crescent :: quarter :

   _ _ _ _

4. dusk : midnight :: midnight :

   d _ _ n

5. summer : autumn :: winter :

   s _ _ _ _ g

Science Analogies

Science: Sequence 5

Use the clue to fill in the missing letters in the last word in each analogy.

1. rubbing : friction :: friction :
    h _ _ _
2. sunlight : plant :: plant :
    h _ _ b _ _ ore
3. seeds : mouse :: mouse :
    h _ _ k
4. caterpillar : cocoon :: cocoon :
    m _ _ _
5. plant : herbivore :: herbivore :
    c _ _ n _ _ o _ e

Science: Part/Whole 1

Fill in the best choice to complete each analogy.

1. baleen : whale :: fangs :
    _____
2. mane : lion :: antlers :
    _____
3. claws : cat :: talons :
    _____
4. horn : rhino :: shell :
    _____
5. camel : hump :: elephant :
    _____

deer trunk tortoise snake eagle

Science: Part/Whole 2

Draw a line to match the word to the analogy.

1. cone : pine :: acorn :
2. leaf : maple :: needle :
3. bill : duck :: teeth :
4. teeth : beaver :: claws :
5. proton : atom :: DNA :

**cell
lobster
fir
alligator
oak**

Science: Part/Whole 3

Fill in the missing letters.

1. arms : starfish :: stinger : r _ _
2. flipper : seal :: antler : d _ _ r
3. fin : shark :: tusk : w _ _ r _ _
4. stripes : tiger :: spots :
    l _ _ p _ r _
5. fur : rabbit :: scales : sn _ _ _

Science Analogies

Science: Part/Whole 4

Unscramble the last word to complete the analogy.

1. fulcrum : lever :: wind :

   _____ rericahun

2. crest : wave :: rope :

   _____ peully

3. moraine : glacier :: trunk :

   _____ tere

4. leaf : herb :: root :

   _____ lantp

5. shell : snail :: feather :

   _____ idrb

Science: Part/Whole 5

Circle the best choice to complete each analogy.

1. leg : animal :: leaf :

   green   lettuce   plant

2. caldera : volcano :: equator :

   planet   equal   poles

3. pole : magnet :: face :

   crystal   flat   edge

4. plate : crust :: tree :

   pine   forest   trunk

5. antenna : ant :: whiskers :

   walrus   smooth   prickly

Science: Greek & Latin Roots 1

Write the word from the box that completes each analogy.

1. distance : telescope :: color :

   _____

2. microphone : sound ::

   microscope : _____

3. photograph : mark ::

   photosynthesis : _____

4. cardiology : heart :: psychology :

   _____

5. biome : ecosystem :: abiotic :

   _____

make	mind	nonliving
spectroscope		sight

Science: Greek & Latin Roots 2

Draw a line to match the word to the analogy.

1. star : interstellar :: galaxy :

2. solar : sun :: lunar :

3. stellar : star :: solar :

4. terrestrial : land :: celestial :

5. conduct : lead :: navigate :

moon
sail
sky
sun
intergalactic

Science Analogies

Science: Greek & Latin Roots 3

Fill in the missing letters.

1. geosphere : earth :: atmosphere :

   a _ _

2. hydrosphere : water :: geosphere :

   e _ _ _ h

3. atmosphere : air :: biosphere :

   l _ _ _

4. seismology : earthquake ::

   oceanography : o _ _ _ n

5. geology : earth :: vulcanology :

   v _ _ c _ n _

Science: Greek & Latin Roots 4

On your own paper, write the following analogies in words. (Example: biology : life :: geology : earth is written as "biology is to life as geology is to earth".)

1. chronometer : time ::

   thermometer : heat

2. photograph : mark ::

   photosynthesis : make

3. cycle : circle :: phobia : fear

4. geology : earth :: hydrology :

   water

5. optical : eye :: audible : ear

Science: Greek & Latin Roots 5

Circle the best choice to complete each analogy.

1. seismology : earthquakes :: geology :	life	stars	earth
2. mammology : mammals :: zoology :	plants	animals	parks
3. horticulture : cultivation :: botany :	plants	clothes	animals
4. cosmology : universe :: astronomy :	earth	fortunes	stars
5. climatology : climate :: meteorology :	meteorites	ecology	weather
6. physiology : physical :: psychology :	vocal	mental	social
7. geologist : earth :: biologist :	life	weather	stars
8. allergist : allergies :: cardiologist :	stomach	feet	heart

Science Analogies

Science: Object/Class 1

Match the word to the analogy.

1. shark : fish :: seal : _____
2. eagle : bird :: tortoise : _____
3. bacteria : living :: basalt : _____
4. fern : plant :: beetle : _____
5. mushroom : fungus ::

   redwood : _____

   a. animal   b. tree
   c. reptile   d. nonliving
   e. mammal

Science: Object/Class 2

Fill in the correct word from the box to complete the analogy.

1. humpback : whale :: tiger :

   _____

2. lion : feline :: wolf :

   _____

3. mouse : herbivore :: hawk :

   _____

4. snake : reptile :: frog :

   _____

5. camel : domesticated ::

   hippopotamus : _____

canine	amphibian	wild
carnivore		feline

Science: Object/Class 3

Use the clue to fill in
the missing letters.

1. monkey : mammal :: shark :

   _ _ s _

2. frog : amphibian :: lizard :

   r _ _ _ _ e

3. water : nonliving :: germ :

   l _ _ i _ g

4. spider : animal :: daisy :

   _ _ a _ t

5. pine : tree :: toadstool :

   f _ _ _ _ s

Science: Object/Class 4

Use the clue to unscramble the last
word in each analogy.

1. lever : machine :: hurricane :

   sormt _____

2. sun : star :: pulley : chaeinm

   _____

3. steam : gas :: ice : liods

   _____

4. snake : vertebrate :: worm :

   vbraterteine _____

5. snail : exoskeleton :: dog :

   eseleonktndo

   _____

Geography Analogies

Geography: Part/Whole 1

Circle the best choice to complete the analogy.

1. bank : stream :: shore :

   coast   lake

2. neighborhood : city :: city :

   state   Denver

3. city : state :: state :

   county   country

4. country : continent :: continent :

   hemisphere island

5. summit : mountain :: bed :

   bottom   river

Geography: Part/Whole 2

Match each relationship to the correct analogy.

1. ridge : ocean :: mountains : _____

2. river : valley :: current : _____

3. path : garden :: trail : _____

4. house : block :: block : _____

5. province : nation :: town : _____

   a. neighborhood
   b. ocean
   c. state
   d. wilderness
   e. land

Geography: Part/Whole 3

Use the clue to fill in the missing letters.

1. tree : forest :: dunes : d _ _ _ _ t

2. ice : glacier :: water : r _ _ _ r

3. stalactite : cave :: crater :

   v _ _ _ _ o

4. forest : biosphere :: lake :

   hy _ _ _ s _ _ _ re

Geography: Part/Whole 4

Unscramble the word to complete the analogy.

1. seasons : climate :: precipitation :

   _____ aterhwe

2. population : census :: area :

   _____ rvseuy

3. grass : plains :: cactus :

   _____ edtser

4. valley : hills :: canyon :

   _____ lautepa

5. stream : river :: pond :

   _____ aekl

Geography Analogies

Geography: Part/Whole 5

Circle the missing word.

1. neighborhood : city :: block : housesquareneighborhood

2. road : country :: street : ohrtownmainpavedturn

3. state : region :: region : westcountrylargewontrs

4. trench : ocean :: gorge : peakdeepmountainsflat

5. farm : country :: factory : manufacturingautocity

Geography: Object/Class 1

Fill in the correct word from the box.

1. Nile : river :: Arctic : _____

2. Antarctica : continent :: Amazon : _____

3. Mississippi : river :: Sahara : _____

4. California : state :: Canada : _____

5. Mediterranean : sea :: Monterey : _____

| desert |
| bay |
| nation |
| river |
| ocean |

Geography: Object/Class 2

Unscramble the word to complete each analogy.

1. Asia : continent :: India : _____ nnioat

2. France : nation :: French : _____ ngugeala

3. Rhine : river :: Alps : _____ untinsamo

4. equator : latitude :: Prime Meridian : _____ gndeitulo

5. Nebraska : state :: Platte : _____ verri

Geography Analogies

Geography: Object/Class 3

On your own paper, write the following analogies in words. (Example: Denali : mountain :: Rio Grande : river is written as "Denali is to mountain as Rio Grande is to river".)

1. Maui : island :: Everest :

   mountain

2. Pacific : ocean :: Baja : peninsula

3. Africa : continent :: Hawaii :

   island

4. Mojave : desert :: Atlantic : ocean

5. Erie : lake :: Columbia : river

Geography: Object/Class 4

Match to complete the analogy.

1. Hudson : bay :: Colorado : ____

2. Chicago : city :: Spain : ____

3. Australia : continent :: Maui :

   ____

4. Atlantic : ocean :: Danube : ____

5. Caribbean : sea :: Appalachians :

   ____

   a. river   b. nation
   c. mountains   d. island
   e. state

Geography: Object/Class 5

Fill in the missing letters.

1. Antigua : island ::

   Red : _ _ a

2. Black : forest :: Tigris : r _ _ _ r

3. London : city :: UK : na _ _ _ _

4. Germany : nation :: Europe :

   c _ _ t _ n _ n _

5. Spain : nation :: Madrid : c _ _ _

Geography: Object/Place 1

Circle the best choice.

1. Golden Gate : San Francisco ::

   Grand Canyon :

   park   river   Arizona

2. Big Ben : London :: Eiffel Tower :

   Paris   famous   France

3. Arches : Utah :: Yosemite :

   waterfall   scenic   California

4. Hoover Dam : Nevada ::

   Vesuvius :

   Italy   Naples   volcano

Geography Analogies

Geography: Object/Place 2

Match the best word to each analogy.

1. kangaroo : Australia :: bison :

   ____

2. Harvard : USA :: Oxford : ____

3. tiger : India :: lion : ____

4. Altamira Cave : Spain ::

   Carlsbad Caverns : ____

5. camel : North Africa :: albatross :

   ____

   a. Africa   b. USA
   c. England
   d. Galapagos Islands   e. USA

Geography: Object/Place 3

Unscramble the last word to complete each analogy.

1. buzzards : Hinckley :: swallows :

   _____ santiraoCp

2. Parthenon : Athens :: Forum :

   _____ moRe

3. White House : Washington, D.C. ::

   Empire State Building :

   _____ ewN roYk

4. iceberg : arctic :: Kilauea :

   _____ waHiai

5. Stonehenge : England :: pyramids :

   _____ ygtpE

Geography: Object/Place 4

Fill in the missing letters.

1. tractor : farm :: elevator : c _ _ y

2. ship : ocean :: railroad : l _ _ d

3. street : city :: highway : st _ _ e

4. tortoise : desert :: turtle : p _ _ _

5. cactus : desert :: fir :

   m _ _ _ t _ _ n _

Geography: Object/Place 5

Unscramble the last word to complete each analogy.

1. spruce : forest :: kelp :

   _____ oance

2. chicken : farm :: eagle :

   _____ mtunnaios

3. fountain : city :: well :

   _____ ntrcoyu

4. bear : mountains :: trout :

   _____ trsema

5. penguin : Antarctica :: ostrich :

   _____ riAafc

Geography Analogies

Geography: Object/ Description 1

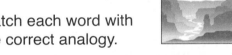

On your own paper, write the following analogies in words. (Example: ocean : large :: lake : small is written as "ocean is to large as lake is to small".)

1. Arctic : cold :: Sahara : hot
2. metropolis : large :: village : small
3. rain forest : wet :: desert : dry
4. plains : flat :: mountains : steep
5. urban : industrial :: rural : agricultural

Geography: Object/ Description 2

Fill in the best word to complete each analogy.

1. island : small :: continent : _____
2. ocean : large :: sea : _____
3. mountains : jagged :: hills : _____
4. cactus : spiny :: moss : _____
5. weather : day :: climate : _____

velvety	**small**	**decade**
rolling	**large**	

Geography: Object/ Description 3

Match each word with the correct analogy.

1. cars : personal :: trains : ____
2. mesa : flat-top :: mountain : ____
3. stream : narrow :: river : ____
4. slope : gentle :: cliff : ____
5. trench : deep :: mountain : ____

a. steep   b. public
c. wide   d. high
e. peak

Geography: Object/ Description 4

Fill in the missing letters.

1. mountain : cool :: rain forest : _ _ _ m
2. grasslands : fertile :: badlands : b _ _ _ _ n
3. plateau : high :: basin : l _ _
4. lake : collecting :: stream : dr _ _ n _ _ g
5. delta : deposited :: valley : e _ _ d _ d

Health Analogies

Health: Object/Class 1

Fill in the missing letters.

1. walking : fitness :: vegetables :

   nu _ _ it _ _ n

2. potato : carbohydrate :: fish :

   p _ _ t _ _ n

3. cheese : dairy :: cereal :

   gr _ _ _ s

4. oats : grains :: milk : d _ _ _ y

5. peach : fruit :: carrot :

   v _ _ _ t _ _ le

Health: Object/Class 2

Unscramble the last word in each analogy.

1. honey : sugar :: butter :

   _____ aft

2. dairy : nutrition :: swimming :

   _____ tsnefis

3. milk : calcium :: cereal :

   _____ rbfie

4. broccoli : vegetable :: apple :

   _____ utifr

5. wheat : grains :: buttermilk :

   _____ ayird

Health: Part/Whole 1

Fill in the blanks with the missing word.

1. knee : leg :: elbow : _____

2. wrist : hand :: ankle : _____

3. neck : head :: waist : _____

4. shoulder : arm :: hip : _____

5. pupil : eye :: crown : _____

| leg | torso | foot | tooth | arm |

Health: Part/Whole 2

Draw a line to match the word with the analogy.

1. chamber : heart :: lobe :

2. roof : mouth :: canal :

3. cochlea : ear :: ribs :

4. lid : eye :: ribs :

5. knuckles : fingers :: elbows :

**chest
skeleton
arms
ear
lung**

Health Analogies

Health: Part/Whole 3

Circle the missing word to complete the analogy.

1. iris : eye :: finger :   armgonefoothandtoeelbowkneww

2. toe : foot :: knee :   legheadneckoranapplbana

3. skull : head :: vertebra :   toeearneckearmouthstngbackbone

4. tongue : mouth :: nostril :   pupiliristongyenosepalettetoothcanine

5. drum : ear :: jaw :   eartoeelbowkjneeskullnoseeyehairarnm

---

Health: Object/Function & Object/Description 1

Fill in the word from the box that completes each analogy.

1. hands : hold :: feet : _____

2. muscles : move :: heart : _____

3. tendons : attach :: bladder : _____

4. lungs : breathe :: brain : _____

5. kidneys : filter :: arteries : _____

| pipe |
| pump |
| control |
| stand |
| collect |

Health: Object/Function & Object/Description 2

Match the best word to each analogy.

1. resistance : strength :: stretching : ____   a. oxygen

2. repetition : endurance :: resistance : ____   b. restoration

3. drink : water :: breath : ____   c. strength

4. talk : communication :: laugh : ____   d. expression

5. food : energy :: sleep : ____   e. flexibility

Health Analogies

Health: Object/Function & Object/Description 3

Unscramble the word to complete the analogy.

1. vegetables : healthy :: donuts :
   _____ atfinteng

2. biking : fast :: hiking :
   _____ wlso

3. ball : throw :: bat :
   _____ igswn

4. television : passive :: skating :
   _____ taciev

5. bandage : protect :: soap :
   _____ dieficsnt

Health: Object/Function & Object/Description 4

Circle the best choice.

1. nerve : communicate :: stomach :
   digest   mouth   tongue

2. teeth : chew :: saliva :
   liquid   mouth   dissolve

3. skin : protect :: blood :
   red   deliver   type

4. skeleton : support :: knees :
   bend   legs   know

5. eyes : see :: nose :
   hear   know   smell

Health: Object/Function & Object/Description 5

Use the clue to fill in the missing letters.

1. tears : moisten :: perspiration :
   _ _ _ l

2. tongue : taste :: ear :
   b _ l _ _ c _

3. nutrition : health :: exercise :
   _ i _ _ _ s _

4. bed : sleep :: table : e _ _

5. park : play :: library : r _ _ _

Health: Various Skills 1

Fill in with a word from the box to complete the analogy.

1. internal : external :: inside :
   _____

2. healthy : sick :: strong :
   _____

3. play : watch :: participant :
   _____

4. happy : sad :: energetic :
   _____

weak	spectator
tired	outside

Health Analogies

Health: Various Skills 2

Draw a line to match the word to the analogy.

1. microscopic : tiny :: large :

2. resonance : echo :: graph :

3. physical : body :: psychological :

4. emotions : feelings :: ideas :

5. nutrition : food :: exercise :

activity
thoughts
mind
big
chart

Health: Various Skills 3

Fill in the missing letters.

1. sea : see :: herd : h _ _ _ d

2. flew : flu :: horse : h _ _ _ _ e

3. heel : heal :: feet : _ _ _ t

4. deer : dear :: here : _ _ _ r

5. knows : nose :: I : e _ _

Health: Various Skills 4

Unscramble the last word in each analogy.

1. here : hear :: site :

   _____ tigsh

2. safe : dangerous :: harmless :

   _____ rdhazusao

3. nontoxic : harmless :: toxic :

   _____ mulfhar

4. tow : toe :: soar :

   _____ osre

5. necessary : unnecessary ::
   healthy :

   _____ elyuhhtna

Health: Various Skills 5

Circle the best choice.

1. chew : crush :: hinge :

   door   steel   bend

2. skeleton : framework :: network :

   system   work   restrain

3. visible : seen :: audible :

   auditorium   touchable   heard

4. elimination : removal ::
   respiration :

   breathing   digestion
   movement

5. circulation : flow :: joint :

   skull   knee   meeting

Art & Music Analogies

Art & Music: Part/Whole & Object/Class 1

Circle the best choice.

1. peg : cello :: pedal :

    horn   volume   piano

2. stick : drum :: bow :

    violin   strings   rosin

3. violinist : orchestra :: trumpeter :

    player   metallic   band

4. president : company :: conductor :

    school   orchestra   hospital

Art & Music: Part/Whole & Object/Class 2

Fill in the analogy with a word from the box.

1. stroke : painting :: note :

    _____

2. landscape : painting :: concerto :

    _____

3. cello : strings :: trumpet :

    _____

4. clarinet : woodwind :: xylophone :

    _____

| composition   brass |
| chord   percussion |

Art & Music: Part/Whole & Object/Class 3

Match the word to the correct analogy.

1. symphony : composition ::
    portrait : _____

2. pianist : musician :: ballerina :
    _____

3. aria : opera :: lights : _____

4. actors : play :: singers : _____

5. singers : opera :: dancers : _____

    a. ballet
    b. opera
    c. dancer
    d. painting
    e. stage

Art & Music: Part/Whole & Object/Class 4

Fill in the missing letters.

1. tuba : brass :: oboe :
    w _ _ d _ _ _ ds

2. reed : bassoon :: slide :
    t _ _ _ b _ _ e

3. brass : band :: strings :
    o _ _ h _ _ t _ _

4. mouthpiece : trumpet :: bridge :
    c _ _ _ _

5. Renoir : Impressionist :: Warhol :
    P _ p

Art & Music Analogies

Art & Music: Part/Whole & Object/Class 5

Circle the missing word that completes each analogy.

1. script : play :: score :   symphony   story   painting

2. perspective : painting :: harmony :   prose   discord   music

3. counterpoint : music :: texture :   rough   bark   painting

4. melody : music :: step :   dance   leap   steppe

5. rest : pausing :: beat :   stopping   acting   beet

Art & Music: Object/Function & Object/Description 1

Circle the missing word.

1. charcoal : dry :: watercolor :   wetundgawpolbnnuct

2. wax : bind :: water :   paintwatecolorthincharcoalpencil

3. pigment : mineral :: acrylic :   vintwilloplastichardsoftmediumdraft

4. pencil : draw :: watercolor :   reddryhatchpaintblueorange

5. painting : decoration :: play :   educentertainmentchninfotosme

---

Art & Music: Object/Function & Object/Description 2

Draw a line to match the word to the analogy.

1. drum : beat :: rattle :   **ring**

2. string : vibrate :: bell :   **words**

3. landscape : scene :: portrait :   **medium**

4. flowers : subject :: watercolor :   **person**

5. script : story :: lines :   **shake**

Art & Music Analogies

Art & Music: Object/Function & Object/Description 3

Circle the best choice.

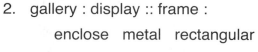

1. model : pose :: crayon :
   color   wax   red

2. gallery : display :: frame :
   enclose   metal   rectangular

3. bronze : casting :: marble :
   limestone   white   carving

4. charcoal : draw :: glue :
   attach   sticky   liquid

5. watercolors : wet :: pastels :
   dry   metal   sticky

Art & Music: Object/Function & Object/Description 4

Fill in the missing letters.

1. painting : picture :: bust :

   _ _ u _ _ t _ _ e

2. play : performance :: paintings :

   e _ _ _ b _ _

3. pencil : draw :: violin : p _ _ _

4. pastel : medium :: mountains :

   _ _ b _ _ _ t

Art & Music: Object/Function & Object/Description 5

Unscramble the last word in each analogy.

1. person : subject :: acrylics :
   _____ memdiu

2. brush : paint :: plate :
   _____ rtinp

3. director : play :: conductor :
   _____ ynmsphoy

4. set : play :: canvas :
   _____ intipnag

5. trumpet : metal :: violin :
   _____ odow

Art & Music: Antonyms, Synonyms, Homophones 1

Circle the best choice to complete each analogy.

1. black : white :: smooth :
   glossy   polished   rough

2. silence : sound :: loud :
   noise   soft   deafening

3. slow : fast :: wet :
   dry   damp   water

4. colorful : gray :: fancy :
   ornate   carved   plain

5. detailed : simplified :: foreground :
   background   front   close

Art & Music Analogies

Art & Music: Antonyms, Synonyms, Homophones 2

Fill in the correct word from the box for each analogy.

1. vertical : horizontal :: narrow :

   _____

2. land : sea :: landscape :

   _____

3. positive : negative :: background :

   _____

4. low : high :: light :

   _____

seascape	foreground
dark	wide

Art & Music: Antonyms, Synonyms, Homophones 3

Draw a line to match the word to the analogy.

1. smooth : rough :: straight :

2. horizontal : vertical :: thick :

3. band : banned :: base :

4. aisle : isle :: beet :

5. story : prose :: melody :

6. waltz : dance :: carve :

beat	tune	curved
sculpt	thin	bass

Art & Music: Antonyms, Synonyms, Homophones 4

Fill in the missing letters.

1. choral : coral :: hew : _ _ e

2. color : hue :: light :

   br _ _ _ _ n _ _ s

3. crimson : red :: ultramarine :

   b _ _ _

4. emerald : green :: golden :

   y _ _ _ _ w

Art & Music: Antonyms, Synonyms, Homophones 5

Unscramble the last word in each analogy.

1. fast : slow :: short :

   _____ nogl

2. solo : alone :: duet :

   _____ prai

3. theme : idea :: variation :

   _____ cnehag

4. inversion : reverse :: tempo :

   _____ sedpe

Math Analogies

Math: Sequence & Number 1

Circle the best choice.

1. first : second :: third :

     three   fourth   ordinal

2. one : two :: six :

     seven   cardinal   sixth

3. A : B :: C :

     letter   fourth   D

4. one : first :: two :

     cardinal   second   three

5. 4 : four :: 9 :

     ninth   nine   numeral

Math: Sequence & Number 2

Draw a line to match each word to the correct analogy.

1. tenth : ten :: hundredth :

2. 120 : 121 :: 130 :

3. 1,000 : 1,001 :: 10,000 :

4. 999 : 1,000 :: 9,999 :

5. 1,000 : thousand :: 1,000,000 :

10,000
million
131
hundred
10,001

Math: Sequence & Number 3

Underline the correct number.

1. 5 : fifth :: 7 :

     seveneightseventhnine

2. fifth : fourth :: third :

     fourththreesecondthree

3. 1 : first :: 6 :

     sixthsixnumeralfifthfour

4. eleven : thirteen :: fifteen :

     sixteenseventeenfifteenth

5. 10 : ten :: 20 :

     twenty-onethirtytwentyforty

Math: Sequence & Number 4

Fill in the missing letters.

1. 100 : hundred :: 100,000 :

     h _ _ d _ _ d th _ _ s _ _ d

2. 99 : hundred :: 999,999 :

     m _ _ _ _ _ n

3. 29 : thirty :: 999 : t _ _ _ _ _ _ d

4. 70 : eighty :: 90 : h _ _ d _ _ d

5. 59 : sixty :: 89 : _ _ n_ t _

Math Analogies

Math: Sequence & Number 5

Complete each analogy with the next item in the sequence or the correct relationship.

1. 11 : 12 :: 100,000 :

    _____

2. 15 : 150 :: 150 : _____

3. one : ten :: ten : _____

4. 1,000,000 : million ::

    1,000,000,000 : _____

5. abcde : edcba :: vwxyz :

    _____

Math: Pattern 1

Circle the best choice to complete the pattern.

1. ABA : BAB :: BCB :

    CBC   BBC   CCB

2. ddb : bbd :: cca :

    caa   aca   aac

3. BbB : CcC :: DdD :

    EEE   eee   EeE

4. fff : ggg :: lll :

    nnn   eee   mmm

5. XOX : xox :: OXO :

    OOO   oxo   xxx

Math: Pattern 2

Fill in each analogy with the correct term from the box.

1. 1A : 2B :: 3C : 4 _____

2. 1, 11 : 2, 22 :: 7, 77 : _____

3. aaAA : ccCC :: eeEE : _____

4. aBcD : bCdE :: gHiJ : _____

5. MmmM : NnnN :: QqqQ : _____

ggGG	hIjK	RrrR
D	8, 88	

Math: Pattern 3

Match each term to the correct analogy.

1. 1A1A : 2A2A :: 5A5A : _____

2. 1010 : 100100 :: 10001000 :

    _____

3. 11aa : 22bb :: 77gg : _____

4. #$: #$# :: ##$$: _____

5. I : II :: X : _____

    a. 88hh
    b. ##$$##
    c. XX
    d. 1000010000
    e. 6A6A

Math Analogies

Math: Pattern 4

Fill in the missing letters.

1. 2, 4, 6, 8 : even :: 1, 3, 5, 7 : o _ _

2. 5, 10, 15 : fives :: 10, 20, 30 : t _ _ _

3. 1, 2, 3 : cardinal :: first, second, third : _ r _ _ _ al

4. 1, 2, 3 : natural :: -1, 0, 1 : _ n _ _ _ er

5. 1, 2, 3 : natural :: $\frac{1}{2}, \frac{1}{4}, \frac{1}{8}$: _ a _ _ _ n _ l

Math: Pattern 5

Circle the best match to complete each analogy.

1. 3, 6, 9, 12 : multiples of 3 :: 6, 12, 18, 24 :

    multiples of 6   multiples of 2

2. 1, 4, 7, 10 : plus three :: 1, 6, 11, 16 :

    plus two   plus five   plus ten

3. 0.1, 0.2, 0.3 : $\frac{1}{10}, \frac{2}{10}, \frac{3}{10}$ :: 1, 2, 3 :

    $\frac{10}{10}, \frac{20}{10}, \frac{30}{10}$ $\frac{1}{4}, \frac{2}{4}, \frac{3}{4}$

Math: Measurement 1

Read each analogy and then write it on your own paper in analogy notation using colons.

1. L is to liter as mL is to milliliter

2. centi is to hundredth as milli is to thousandth

3. Celcius is to temperature as gram is to weight

4. meter is to length as liter is to volume

5. staple is to millimeter as highway is to kilometer

Math Analogies

Math: Measurement 2

Circle each missing word.

1. inch : foot :: foot :

    yard   inch   mile

2. foot : yard :: yard :

    mile   inch   yard

3. cup : pint :: pint :

    cup   quart   gallon

4. pint : quart :: quart :

    gallon   quart   pint

5. inch : standard :: paperclip :

    nonstandard   inch   gram

Math: Measurement 3

Complete the analogy with a word from the box.

1. five : number :: inch : _____

2. inch : length :: ounce : _____

3. second : minute :: minute :

    _____

4. minute : hour :: hour : _____

5. hour : day :: day : _____

day	weight	month
hour	unit	

Math: Measurement 4

Draw a line to match the word to the analogy.

1. year : time :: ton :

2. degree : temperature :: mile :

3. mile : kilometer :: gallon :

4. ounce : gram :: inch :

5. meter : kilometer :: gram :

liter
kilogram
centimeter
distance
weight

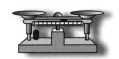

Math: Measurement 5

Fill in the missing letters.

1. C : Celsius :: F :

    F _ hr _ _ h _ i _

2. m : meter :: km : ki _ _ _ e _ _ r

3. mm : millimeter :: cm :

    c _ _ ti _ _ t _ r

4. kg : kilogram :: g : g _ _ m

5. mm : millimeter :: mg :

    m _ _ _ i _ _ a _

Math Analogies

Math: Geometry 1

On your own paper, write the following analogies in words. (Example: rectangle: cylinder :: triangle : cone is written as "rectangle is to cylinder as triangle is to cone".)

1. acute : obtuse :: less : more

2. square : cube :: triangle : pyramid

3. triangle : cone :: circle : sphere

4. rectangle : rectangular prism ::

    triangle : triangular prism

Math: Geometry 2

Fill in the missing letters to complete each analogy.

1. isosceles : equilateral :: rectangle :

    sq _ _ _ e

2. acute : equilateral :: obtuse :

    sc _ _ _ ne

3. obtuse angle : parallelogram ::

    right angle : r _ _ t _ _ _ le

4. polygon : closed curve :: square :

    q _ _ _ ri _ _ t _ _ a _

Math: Geometry 3

Unscramble the last word in each analogy.

1. vertex : angle :: end point :

    _____ ayr

2. 1 end point : ray :: 2 end points :

    _____

    neli smteneg

3. segment : limited :: line :

    _____ snesdle

4. inside : outside :: interior :

    _____ tereioxr

Math: Geometry 4

Circle the best choice.

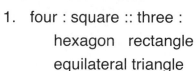

1. four : square :: three :
    hexagon   rectangle
    equilateral triangle

2. hexagon : shape :: five :
    six   number   half

3. protractor : angle :: ruler :
    line segment   measure
    count

4. triangle : three :: pentagon :
    ninth   building   five

5. seven : heptagon :: eight :
    quadrangle   octagon   triangle

Math Analogies

Math: Geometry 5

Draw a line to match the word to the correct analogy.

1. arc : circle :: line segment :   **square**

2. perimeter : rectangle :: circumference :   **parallel**

3. congruent : equal :: equidistant :   **line**

4. quadrilateral : trapezoid :: parallelogram :   **circle**

5. parallelogram : rhombus :: rhombus :   **rectangle**

Math: Fractions 1

Circle the best choice to complete each analogy.

1. $\frac{1}{5}$: fifth :: $\frac{1}{6}$:   six   seventh   sixth

2. third : $\frac{1}{3}$ :: half : $\frac{1}{4}$ $\frac{1}{2}$ 0.25

3. $\frac{1}{4}$: fourth :: $\frac{1}{7}$:   seventh   eighth   seven

4. $\frac{1}{8}$: $\frac{1}{9}$ :: eighth :   nine   eight   ninth

5. 10 : $\frac{1}{10}$ :: ten :   eleventh   0.01   tenth

Math: Fractions 2

Finish each analogy with a term from the box.

1. 0.5 : $\frac{1}{2}$ :: 0.2 : _____

2. 0.2 : two-tenths :: 0.3 : _____

3. 0.2 : 0.02 :: tenths : _____

4. 0.02 : 0.002 :: hundredths : _____

5. 0.25 : quarter :: 0.5 : _____

> **hundredths**
> **thousandths**
> **half**
> $\frac{1}{5}$
> **three-tenths**

Math Analogies

Math: Fractions 3

Draw a line to match the term to the analogy.

1. $\frac{5}{10}$: half :: $\frac{10}{10}$:

2. $\frac{3}{3}$: whole :: $\frac{1}{3}$:

3. $\frac{2}{4}$: 0.5 :: $\frac{1}{4}$:

4. $\frac{3}{6}$: $\frac{1}{2}$ :: $\frac{3}{12}$:

5. $\frac{1}{2}$: half :: $\frac{1}{4}$:

0.25

third

quarter

$\frac{1}{4}$

whole

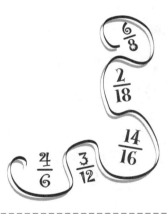

Math: Fractions 4

Fill in the missing letters.

1. $\frac{3}{9}$: third :: $\frac{2}{10}$: f _ _ _ h

2. $\frac{2}{12}$: sixth :: $\frac{3}{21}$: s _ _ _ _ th

3. $\frac{10}{70}$: seventh :: $\frac{10}{30}$: t _ _ _ d

4. 0.70 : seven-tenths :: 0.90 : n _ _ e-t _ _ _ h _

5. 0.8 : tenths :: 0.008 : th _ _ s _ _ d _ _ s

Math: Fractions 5

Circle the best choice to complete each analogy.

1. 0.7 : $\frac{7}{10}$ :: 0.07 :   7 $\frac{7}{10}$ $\frac{7}{100}$

2. $\frac{7}{9}$: $\frac{14}{18}$ :: $\frac{5}{6}$: $\frac{10}{12}$ $\frac{20}{25}$ $\frac{15}{30}$

3. $\frac{12}{15}$: $\frac{4}{5}$ :: $\frac{6}{9}$: $\frac{1}{2}$ $\frac{4}{5}$ $\frac{2}{3}$

4. 0.17 : $\frac{17}{100}$ :: 0.017 : $\frac{1}{7}$ $\frac{17}{10}$ $\frac{17}{1000}$

5. $\frac{3}{4}$: $\frac{15}{20}$ :: $\frac{7}{8}$: $\frac{22}{44}$ $\frac{34}{98}$ $\frac{35}{40}$

Answer Keys

Solving Analogies: Related Pairs (pg. 2–3)

Set 1 1. antonyms 2. part/whole
3. sequence (order) 4. cause/effect
5. object/action 6. person/action
7. group/member 8. synonyms
9. object/use 10. object/description

Set 2 1. c 2. a 3. d 4. e 5. b

Set 3 1. thin 2. huge 3. two
4. wall 5. reptile

Set 4 1. teaching 2. marker 3. mark
4. tiny 5. school

Set 5 1. laugh 2. sentence 3. acting
4. sixth 5. fry

Set 6 Answers will vary.

Vocabulary Analogies: Object/Characteristic (pg. 4–5)

Set 1 1. purple 2. yellow 3. orange
4. red 5. red

Set 2 1. thorny 2. opaque 3. hard
4. smooth 5. heavy

Set 3 1. cool 2. hot 3. shiny
4. crisp 5. light

Set 4 1. liquid 2. cold 3. strong
4. cool 5. hot

Set 5 1. e 2. d 3. b 4. a 5. c

Vocabulary Analogies: Member/Group (pg. 5–6)

Set 1 1. faculty 2. crowd 3. galaxy
4. pack 5. crew

Set 2 1. collection 2. senate 3. colony
4. audience 5. team

Set 3 1. c 2. a 3. e 4. d 5. b

Set 4 1. tree is to grove as flower is to bed
2. actor is to cast as singer is to chorus
3. chapter is to book as room is to building
4. block is to neighborhood as neighborhood is to city

Set 5 1. band 2. team 3. library
4. herd 5. vineyard

Vocabulary Analogies: Object/Action (pg. 6–7)

Set 1 1. bounce 2. roll 3. hop
4. bound 5. fall

Set 2 1. watch 2. toot 3. rumble
4. stir 5. break

Set 3 1. sniff 2. flow 3. fly
4. creak 5. pelt

Set 4 1. bounce 2. sink 3. spray
4. swim 5. honk

Set 5 1. croak 2. neigh 3. waddle
4. honk 5. pierce

Vocabulary Analogies: Part/Whole (pg. 8–9)

Set 1 1. knife 2. tire 3. belt
4. watch 5. guitar

Set 2 1. e 2. d 3. b 4. c 5. a

Set 3 1. library 2. mouth 3. stadium
4. glove 5. box

Set 4 1. frame is to picture as fence is to yard
2. knob is to drawer as handle is to door
3. piece is to puzzle as letter is to word
4. mattress is to bed as burner is to stove
5. inch is to foot as foot is to mile

Set 5 1. compass 2. music 3. branch
4. roof 5. cabinet

Vocabulary Analogies: Object/Purpose (pg. 9–10)

Set 1 1. T 2. F 3. F 4. T 5. T

Set 2 1. sleep 2. clean 3. drink
4. listen 5. dry

Set 3 1. contain 2. wear 3. hold
4. smell 5. hear

Set 4 1. sew 2. smooth 3. print
4. clean 5. add

Set 5 1. wash 2. drive 3. eat
4. serve 5. cool

Vocabulary Analogies: Synonyms & Antonyms (pg. 10–11)

Set 1 1. level 2. grand 3. glad
4. declare 5. stop

Set 2 1. dislike 2. work 3. woman
4. mother 5. take

Set 3 1. restore   2. site   3. country
       4. loyal   5. winner
Set 4 1. depressed 2. laugh   3. like
       4. take   5. colorless
Set 5 1. near   2. grow   3. mistake
       4. verse   5. little

Vocabulary Analogies: Homophones (pg. 12–13)

Set 1 1. one   2. bear   3. red
       4. bread   5. piece
Set 2 1. passed   2. hair   3. claws
       4. site   5. nose
Set 3 1. oar is to ore as soar is to sore
       2. here is to hear as herd is to heard
       3. heal is to heel as real is to reel
       4. lead is to led as read is to red
       5. peek is to peak as week is to weak
Set 4 1. mane   2. sale   3. rowed
       4. yule   5. reed
Set 5 1. ant   2. carrot   3. for
       4. not   5. roll

Vocabulary Analogies: Suffixes (pg. 13–14)

Set 1 1. perishable 2. worker 3. reader
       4. editor   5. buyer
Set 2 1. active   2. excitement
       3. lifeless   4. fearful 5. bravery
Set 3 1. strength is to strengthen as length is to
          lengthen
       2. light is to lighter as dark is to darker
       3. lucky is to luckier as happy is to
          happier
       4. soft is to softest as hard is to hardest
       5. boy is to boyish as girl is to girlish
Set 4 1. d   2. c   3. e   4. b   5. a
Set 5 1. citizenship 2. sadness 3. sadly
       4. crying   5. division

Vocabulary Analogies: Prefixes (pg. 14–16)

Set 1 1. rewrite   2. incomplete
       3. disappear   4. nonprofit
       5. refund
Set 2 1. preheat   2. interstate
       3. overspend   4. misunderstand
       5. recopy
Set 3 1. submarine   2. semifinal
       3. untrue   4. underground
       5. overprice

Set 4 1. impatient   2. imperfect
       3. irregular   4. impossible
       5. inattention
Set 5 1. precut   2. repay
       3. unsolved   4. outperform
       5. biannually

Vocabulary Analogies: Greek & Latin Roots (pg. 16–17)

Set 1 1. sound   2. three   3. sight
       4. small   5. life
Set 2 1. rider   2. speak   3. corners
       4. broken   5. foot   6. solid
       7. writing   8. body
Set 3 1. e   2. b   3. d   4. a   5. c
Set 4 1. death   2. moon   3. in
       4. father   5. out
Set 5 1. stretch   2. give   3. pressure
       4. more   5. hear

Vocabulary Analogies: Clipped Words (pg. 17–18)

Set 1 1. memorandum   2. influenza
       3. veterinarian 4. laboratory
       5. Internet
Set 2 1. helicopter   2. teenager
       3. fanatic   4. caravan
       5. dormitory
Set 3 1. d   2. c   3. e   4. a   5. b
Set 4 1. automobile   2. stereophonic
       3. necktie   4. doctor   5. omnibus
Set 5 1. graduate   2. hippopotamus
       3. submarine   4. professor
       5. cellular

Vocabulary Analogies: Acronyms (pg. 19–20)

Set 1 1. possible   2. union   3. jockey
       4. ship   5. recorder
Set 2 1. d   2. a   3. e   4. b   5. c
Set 3 1. number   2. imaging   3. quotient
       4. service 5. information
Set 4 1. officer 2. intelligence 3. head
       4. video   5. grade
Set 5 1. memory   2. announced
       3. service 4. apparatus
       5. team   6. league
       7. assistant 8. department

Vocabulary Analogies: Portmanteau Words (pg. 20–21)

Set 1   1. commercial   2. friend
        3. emoticon   4. lunch
        5. documentary
Set 2   1. e   2. d   3. a   4. b   5. c
Set 3   1. e   2. c   3. d   4. b   5. a
Set 4   1. commercial   2. comedy
        3. language   4. mash
        5. slop
Set 5   1. squiggle is to wiggle as telethon is to
           marathon
        2. pulsar is to star as bionic is to electronic
        3. stagflation is to inflation as netiquette
           is to etiquette
        4. swipe is to sweep as splatter is to
           splash
        5. carjack is to hijack as chillax is to relax

Grammar Analogies: Irregular Verb Forms (pg. 22–23)

Set 1   1. were   2. caught   3. froze
        4. brought 5. got
Set 2   1. had   2. flew   3. drank
        4. cut   5. bit
Set 3   1. ate   2. bled   3. drank
        4. felt   5. broke
Set 4   1. lay   2. said   3. sold
        4. shook   5. spun
Set 5   1. grew   2. made   3. rose
        4. took   5. meant

Grammar Analogies: Parts of Speech (pg. 23–24)

Set 1   1. lazily   2. nicely   3. needlessly
        4. internally   5. delightfully
Set 2   1. verb   2. adverb   3. noun
        4. adjective   5. adverb
Set 3   1. well   2. slowly   3. merrily
        4. greedy   5. crazy
Set 4   1. d   2. c   3. e   4. b   5. a
Set 5   1. adverb   2. adjective   3. noun
        4. verb   5. adjective

Phonics Analogies: Long & Short Vowels (pg. 25–26)

Set 1   1. pane   2. plane   3. rat
        4. stare   5. bit   6. hop
        7. snipe   8. win
Set 2   1. ride   2. slime   3. prime
        4. spine   5. pine
Set 3   1. gripe   2. site   3. globe
        4. slope   5. tote
Set 4   1. hug is to huge as cut is to cute
        2. slat is to slate as scrap is to scrape
        3. gap is to gape as tap is to tape
        4. ton is to tone as mop is to mope
        5. spit is to spite as fir is to fire
Set 5   1. can   2. fare   3. tape
        4. made   5. fade

Phonics Analogies: Blends & Digraphs (pg. 26–27)

Set 1   1. trend   2. trip   3. fly
        4. glob   5. shore
Set 2   1. snap   2. then   3. trail
        4. shop   5. score
Set 3   1. slid   2. smash   3. plot
        4. knob   5. gray
Set 4   1. land   2. mast   3. bath
        4. wing   5. west   6. hench
        7. booth   8. ting   9. belt
        10. thing
Set 5   1. sl   2. sh   3. sp   4. tr   5. ng

Literature Analogies: Poetic Devices (pg. 28–29)

Set 1   1. horse is to neigh as dog is to
           bow-wow
        2. pig is to oink as duck is to quack
        3. frog is to ribbit as cat is to meow
        4. cow is to moo as sheep is to baa
        5. donkey is to heehaw as chicken is to
           cluck
Set 2   1. e   2. a   3. d   4. b   5. c
Set 3   1. row   2. budge   3. row
        4. mound   5. truck
Set 4   1. pet   2. dad   3. rag
        4. end   5. poem
Set 5   1. brrrrrh 2. ding   3. chug
        4. shhh   5. yuck

Literature Analogies: Narrative Elements
(pg. 29–30)
Set 1 1. setting   2. conflict   3. character
       4. resolution   5. problem
Set 2 1. setting   2. resolution
       3. poverty   4. problem 5. character
Set 3 1. d   2. e   3. a   4. c   5. b
Set 4 1. resolution   2. genre   3. conflict
       4. setting   5. character
Set 5 1. setting   2. resolution
       3. theme   4. genre   5. conflict

Literature Analogies: Parts of a Book
(pg. 30–31)
Set 1 1. book   2. paragraph   3. index
       4. contents   5. beginning
Set 2 1. after   2. subheading 3. book
       4. glossary
Set 3 1. e   2. c   3. b   4. d   5. a
Set 4 1. nonfiction   2. fiction   3. dictionary
       4. diagram   5. globe
Set 5 1. index   2. keyword   3. fiction
       4. sources

Science Analogies: Sequence (pg. 32–33)
Set 1 1. sandstone   2. slate   3. tuff
       4. fossil
Set 2 1. seed is to sprout as sprout is to stem
       2. pollen is to seed as seed is to sprout
       3. leaf is to bud as bud is to flower
       4. light is to photosynthesis as
          photosynthesis is to food
       5. bud is to flower as flower is to fruit
Set 3 1. d   2. e   3. b   4. c   5. a
Set 4 1. sunset   2. new   3. full
       4. dawn   5. spring
Set 5 1. heat   2. herbivore   3. hawk
       4. moth   5. carnivore

Science Analogies: Part/Whole (pg. 33–34)
Set 1 1. snake   2. deer   3. eagle
       4. tortoise 5. trunk
Set 2 1. oak   2. fir   3. alligator
       4. lobster   5. cell
Set 3 1. ray   2. deer   3. walrus
       4. leopard   5. snake
Set 4 1. hurricane   2. pulley   3. tree
       4. plant   5. bird
Set 5 1. plant   2. planet   3. crystal
       4. forest   5. walrus

Science Analogies: Greek & Latin Roots
(pg. 34–35)
Set 1 1. spectroscope   2. sight
       3. make   4. mind
       5. nonliving
Set 2 1. intergalactic   2. moon
       3. sun   4. sky
       5. sail
Set 3 1. air   2. earth
       3. life   4. ocean
       5. volcano
Set 4 1. chronometer is to time as thermometer
          is to heat
       2. photograph is to mark as
          photosynthesis is to make
       3. cycle is to circle as phobia is to fear
       4. geology is to earth as hydrology is to
          water
       5. opitcal is to eye as audible is to ear
Set 5 1. earth   2. animals   3. plants
       4. stars   5. weather   6. mental
       7. life   8. heart

Science Analogies: Object/Class (pg. 36)
Set 1 1. e   2. c   3. d   4. a   5. b
Set 2 1. feline   2. canine   3. carnivore
       4. amphibian   5. wild
Set 3 1. fish   2. reptile   3. living
       4. plant   5. fungus
Set 4 1. storm   2. machine   3. solid
       4. invertebrate 5. endoskeleton

Geography Analogies: Part/Whole
(pg. 37–38)
Set 1 1. lake   2. state   3. country
       4. hemisphere 5. river
Set 2 1. e   2. b   3. d   4. a   5. c
Set 3 1. desert   2. river   3. volcano
       4. hydrosphere
Set 4 1. weather   2. survey   3. desert
       4. plateau   5. lake
Set 5 1. neighborhood   2. town 3. country
       4. mountains   5. city

Geography Analogies: Object/Class
(pg. 38–39)
Set 1 1. ocean   2. river   3. desert
       4. nation   5. bay
Set 2 1. nation   2. language
       3. mountains   4. longitude   5. river

Set 3 1. Maui is to island as Everest is to mountain
2. Pacific is to ocean as Baja is to peninsula
3. Africa is to continent as Hawaii is to island
4. Mojave is to desert as Atlantic is to ocean
5. Erie is to lake as Columbia is to river

Set 4 1. e   2. b   3. d   4. a   5. c

Set 5 1. sea   2. river   3. nation
4. continent   5. city

Geography Analogies: Object/Place (pg. 39–40)

Set 1 1. Arizona   2. Paris   3. California
4. Naples

Set 2 1. b/e   2. c   3. a   4. b/e   5. d

Set 3 1. Capistrano   2. Rome   3. New York
4. Hawaii   5. Eygpt

Set 4 1. city   2. land   3. state
4. pond   5. mountains

Set 5 1. ocean   2. mountains 3. country
4. stream   5. Africa

Geography Analogies: Object/Description (pg. 41)

Set 1 1. Arctic is to cold as Sahara is to hot
2. metropolis is to large as village is to small
3. rain forest is to wet as desert is to dry
4. plains are to flat as mountains are to steep
5. urban is to industrial as rural is to agricultural

Set 2 1. large   2. small   3. rolling
4. velvety   5. decade

Set 3 1. b   2. e   3. c   4. a   5. d

Set 4 1. warm   2. barren   3. low
4. draining   5. eroded

Health Analogies: Object/Class (pg. 42)

Set 1 1. nutrition 2. protein   3. grains
4. dairy   5. vegetable

Set 2 1. fat   2. fitness   3. fiber
4. fruit   5. dairy

Health Analogies: Part/Whole (p. 42–43)

Set 1 1. arm   2. foot   3. torso
4. leg   5. tooth

Set 2 1. lung   2. ear   3. skeleton
4. chest   5. arms

Set 3 1. hand   2. leg   3. backbone
4. nose   5. skull

Health Analogies: Object/Function & Object/Description (pg. 43–44)

Set 1 1. stand   2. pump   3. collect
4. control   5. pipe

Set 2 1. e   2. c   3. a   4. d   5. b

Set 3 1. fattening   2. slow   3. swing
4. active   5. disinfect

Set 4 1. digest   2. dissolve   3. deliver
4. bend   5. smell

Set 5 1. cool   2. balance   3. fitness
4. eat   5. read

Health Analogies: Various Skills (pg. 44–45)

Set 1 1. outside 2. weak   3. spectator
4. tired

Set 2 1. big   2. chart   3. mind
4. thoughts   5. activity

Set 3 1. heard   2. hoarse   3. feat
4. hear   5. eye

Set 4 1. sight   2. hazardous   3. harmful
4. sore   5. unhealthy

Set 5 1. bend   2. system   3. heard
4. breathing   5. meeting

Art & Music Analogies: Part/Whole & Object/Class (pg. 46–47)

Set 1 1. piano   2. violin   3. band
4. orchestra

Set 2 1. chord   2. composition 3. brass
4. percussion

Set 3 1. d   2. c   3. e   4. b   5. a

Set 4 1. woodwinds 2. trombone
3. orchestra   4. cello   5. Pop

Set 5 1. symphony 2. music   3. painting
4. dance   5. acting

Art & Music Analogies: Object/Function & Object/Description (pg. 47–48)

Set 1 1. wet   2. thin   3. plastic
       4. paint   5. entertainment
Set 2 1. shake   2. ring   3. person
       4. medium   5. words
Set 3 1. color   2. enclose   3. carving
       4. attach   5. dry
Set 4 1. sculpture   2. exhibit 3. play
       4. subject
Set 5 1. medium 2. print   3. symphony
       4. painting 5. wood

Art & Music Analogies: Antonyms, Synonyms, Homophones (pg. 48–49)

Set 1 1. rough   2. soft   3. dry
       4. plain   5. background
Set 2 1. wide   2. seascape
       3. foreground 4. dark
Set 3 1. curved   2. thin   3. bass
       4. beat   5. tune   6. sculpt
Set 4 1. hue   2. brightness   3. blue
       4. yellow
Set 5 1. long   2. pair   3. change
       4. speed

Math Analogies: Sequence & Number (pg. 50–51)

Set 1 1. fourth   2. seven   3. D
       4. second   5. nine
Set 2 1. hundred   2. 131   3. 10,001
       4. 10,000   5. million
Set 3 1. seventh   2. second   3. sixth
       4. seventeen 5. twenty
Set 4 1. hundred thousand   2. million
       3. thousand   4. hundred 5. ninety
Set 5 1. 100,001   2. 1,500   3. hundred
       4. billion   5. zyxwv

Math Analogies: Pattern (pg. 51–52)

Set 1 1. CBC   2. aac   3. EeE
       4. mmm   5. oxo
Set 2 1. D   2. 8, 88   3. ggGG
       4. hIjK   5. RrrR
Set 3 1. e   2. d   3. a   4. b   5. c
Set 4 1. odd   2. tens   3. ordinal
       4. integer   5. rational
Set 5 1. multiples of 6   2. plus five
       3. $\frac{10}{10}, \frac{20}{10}, \frac{30}{10}$

Math Analogies: Measurement (pg. 52–53)

Set 1 1. L : liter :: mL : milliliter
       2. centi : hundredth :: milli : thousandth
       3. Celcius : temperature :: gram : weight
       4. meter : length :: liter : volume
       5. staple : millimeter :: highway : kilometer
Set 2 1. yard   2. mile   3. quart
       4. gallon   5. nonstandard
Set 3 1. unit   2. weight   3. hour
       4. day   5. month
Set 4 1. weight   2. distance   3. liter
       4. centimeter 5. kilogram
Set 5 1. Fahrenheit 2. kilometer
       3. centimeter 4. gram   5. milligram

Math Analogies: Geometry (pg. 54–55)

Set 1 1. acute is to obtuse as less is to more
       2. square is to cube as triangle is to pyramid
       3. triangle is to cone as circle is to sphere
       4 rectangle is to rectangular prism as triangle is to triangular prism
Set 2 1. square   2. scalene 3. rectangle
       4. quadrilateral
Set 3 1. ray   2. line segment
       3. endless   4. exterior
Set 4 1. equilateral triangle   2. number
       3. line segment   4. five   5. octagon
Set 5 1. line   2. circle   3. parallel
       4. rectangle   5. square

Math Analogies: Fractions (pg. 55–56)

Set 1 1. sixth   2. $\frac{1}{2}$ 3. seventh
       4. ninth   5. tenth
Set 2 1. $\frac{1}{5}$ 2. three-tenths
       3. hundredths 4. thousandths
       5. half
Set 3 1. whole   2. third   3. 0.25
       4. $\frac{1}{4}$ 5. quarter
Set 4 1. fifth   2. seventh   3. third
       4. nine-tenths 5. thousandths
Set 5 1. $\frac{7}{100}$ 2. $\frac{10}{12}$ 3. $\frac{2}{3}$
       4. $\frac{17}{1000}$ 5. $\frac{35}{40}$